LEADER GUIDE

Abingdon Press
Nashville

Affirm: Leader Guide

Writer: Audrey Wilder
Editor: Sara Galyon

Websites are constantly changing. Although the websites recommended in this resource were checked at the time this unit was developed, we recommend that you double-check all sites to verify that they are still live and that they are still suitable for students before doing an activity.

ISBN: 9781501867736

PACP10537569-01

18 19 20 21 22 23 24 25 26 27 — 10 9 8 7 6 5 4 3 2 1

MANUFACTURED IN THE UNITED STATES OF AMERICA

Contents

About Affirm

Alongside the natural changes taking place in the lives of teens are the stresses and distractions the world brings that can be challenging as they are working out their faith. This is especially true for the all-important time after they say yes to Jesus, whether through confirmation or another way. Their faith is new, exciting, and not yet fully formed. Youth experts recognize this time as a transition from a teen embracing their faith in Jesus Christ to their faith taking hold of them.

Teens need to own their faith, and the way to do that involves thinking critically, asking questions, and practice. Without intentional guidance, many teens have simply dropped out of church.

AFFIRM is designed to be the tool you need to step into the opportunity you have to continue to guide your teens toward a more fully formed faith. As a flexible and customizable six-lesson study, you can place it in your teaching plan when your teens need it most. Because it helps you create space for deeper reflection, it's best used as a retreat or small-group study and, like *Confirm*, encourages parents and mentors to join alongside your teens in this part of their faith journey.

Affirm Resource Kit

Leader Guide

The Leader Guide has everything you need to facilitate six impactful gatherings for continued faith formation. Each lesson includes a parent email, a leader note, and a Theology and Commentary section to provide more information about that week's topic. It is designed to be used in conjunction with the Student Guide. The Leader Guide has five sections:

Connect introduces your group to the theme through either a high- or low-energy activity.

Explore is the part of the lesson that invites teens to chew on the Scripture through creative learning.

Reflect is where teens can process what they've heard and experienced.

Create provides the opportunity to put their learning and experience into tangible practice using creative activities.

Next helps teens take those ideas for practice and put them into their everyday lives.

Student Guide

The AFFIRM STUDENT GUIDE provides engaging opportunities for your teens to take hold of the Spirit's working through the lessons. The creative activities are integral and critical to your teens taking hold of their faith formation in lasting ways. Encourage your teens to think about the week's topic ahead of your youth gathering using the Solo Searching section.

DVD

The Affirm DVD includes six ninety-second, animated videos that are placed within each lesson to deliver and unpack more complex concepts and ideas. Each video is made to clearly communicate, without oversimplifying.

Mentor Guide

One of the best ways to disciple young people is through mentoring. With the Affirm Mentor Guide, adult spiritual friends of teens will be better equipped to walk alongside them as they discover how to follow Jesus for a lifetime. Mentoring sessions are outlined for each of the six lessons.

Parent Guide

The Affirm Parent Guide provides everything parents need to continue partnering with their teens on their ongoing faith journey. Included is helpful information about their teen's faith formation process, opportunity to clarify their own faith and the hopes they have for their teens, and practical ideas for parents to have spiritual conversations with their teens.

1   *The Faith Journey*

Summary

Transformation is the process and journey of becoming more like Christ. While parts of the journey must be traveled alone, we are meant to have companions. This session will help students realize that their pace of transformation is unique to the purpose God has for them, and that the community of faith has a role to play in supporting and encouraging them along the way.

Overview

- **Connect** through a choice of activities that challenge students to explore the practical aspects of transformation.

- **Explore** how Paul encourages the early Christian church to be agents of transformation.

- **Reflect** on what transformation means personally.

- **Create** encouragement for statements to help others in their journey of transformation.

- **Next,** practice becoming a person who lives a transformed life every day.

Anchor Point

Philippians 1:6 — I'm sure about this: the one who started a good work in you will stay with you to complete the job by the day of Christ Jesus.

Supplies

- High-Energy Supplies: transformation object sticky notes
- Low-Energy Supplies: baby and present-day pictures of each participant, posterboard, tape
- Student Guides
- Pencils/pens
- Paper for each student
- Baby Ruth candy bar
- Digital cameras or magazines

Parent Email

Your student is beginning a six-lesson study exploring what it means to affirm their belief in God by living their faith. The goal of these lessons is to help faith practices become a normal part of their everyday routine. Living with Jesus isn't something they tack on to their extracurricular activities, but should be intricately woven into their day-to-day living.

As part of these faith practices, students will have three devotions each week to complete **before** coming to the study with their peers. Some of these devotions will require interacting with you, neighbors, or other congregation members. We encourage you to support your student in the development of these faith practices.

Leader Notes

Change is a constant reality in the lives of adolescents. Transformation may not be a term or concept that is familiar to your students, but they will understand change. It may be helpful for you to continue to remind your students, throughout the lesson, that transformation and change are often used interchangeably. However, the use of transformation in the context of spiritual change is intentional because it points to change on a variety of levels.

Theology and Commentary

The process of becoming perfect in Christ, or "sanctified," is a cornerstone of Wesleyan theology. Specifically, John Wesley put an emphasis on the *process* of transformation. The importance of transformation was not just a theological concept constructed by Wesley, but one rooted in the Holy Scripture. One of the most vivid pictures we have on what transformation looks like is the life of Paul. His life, as revealed through the Book of Acts and the epistles, gives us a window into the ways ups and downs of living a life in service to Christ made him more like Christ.

Paul's ongoing sanctification shaped his ministry and the content of his letters. Forged in his encounter with the risen Christ, his conviction that Christ died and was raised for the salvation of the world gave his voice authority, despite efforts of false teachers to discredit him.

Paul writes to his churches in a manner that is both encouraging and challenging. His belief in the imminent return of Christ gives his letters a sense of urgency. While Paul's death is surrounded in mystery, 2 Timothy feels almost like a farewell address as he describes the lengths to which he has gone for the sake of the gospel. While scholars still debate if Paul actually authored 2 Timothy, the power of the words shows us his commitment to his relationship with fellow believers and ultimately to Christ:

> *I'm already being poured out like a sacrifice to God, and the time of my death is near. I have fought the good fight, finished the race, and kept the faith. At last the champion's wreath that is awarded for righteousness is waiting for me. The Lord, who is the righteous judge, is going to give it to me on that day. He's giving it not only to me but also to all those who have set their heart on waiting for his appearance (2 Timothy 4:6-8).*

4

While Paul's teaching and unwavering faithfulness to the gospel made as many enemies as friends, his friendships were characterized by a shared love for Christ. The decision to follow Christ is, for most westerners, a countercultural commitment, and close relationships with other believers are critical for support, courage, and strength. Paul would not have been able to do all that God intended without the hospitality of Lydia, the friendship of Timothy, or the accountability of Peter. Surrounding ourselves with a community of faith is what gives us support and needed encouragement to follow Jesus faithfully as, together, we are empowered to reflect the image of Christ to the world.

Leader Reflection

Read Philippians 1:3-11 and Acts 9:1-22.

Transformation is a process everyone has experienced in some capacity in their lives. In preparation for this lesson, think back to a single transformative experience in your life. Who was with you? How did God prepare you? What did you need to go through the transformation?

Now, think about the little ways you have been transformed in the past two years. Write down things you are doing now that you didn't imagine you would be doing two years ago.

If you haven't before, consider what has God been doing in you over the past two years to prepare you for what you are facing right now or in the immediate future.

Transformation is both instantaneous and incremental. Your attention to how God is present and active in both instantaneous and incremental moments in your own life will be helpful in recognizing God's activity in the lives of your students.

At times, we can overvalue or emphasize one of these ways of transformation to the exclusion of the other. As you are reflecting on your own transformation experiences and walking with your students through theirs, it's important to honor and lift up both as viable options for spiritual growth.

Be in prayer for your students and your preparation:

- Ask God to open your eyes to transformation experiences within yourself and your students.

- Invite God into relationships or habits in your life that you know need transformation.

- Open your heart to how God will use you as a means of transformation for others.

Connect (6–8 minutes)

High-Energy Option — *Things That Transform*

[Before starting: Using sticky notes, write one of the following transforming processes per note. After the students have settled, provide the following instructions.]

- Seed to Flower

- Caterpillar to Butterfly

- Kernel to Popcorn

- Tadpole to Frog

- Ice to Water

Say: Each of you is getting a sticky note with a word written on it. You will have two minutes to find another person in this room whose sticky note is related to yours. You will be searching for your partner without using words. Using only motions or expressions, you must find the other person who connects with your sticky note.

[Once all the students have found their transformation partner . . .]

Say something like: Take a minute-and-a-half to talk with your partner about what is required for your object to transform.

[Gather the group back together for a brief discussion on the activity.]

Ask:

- What do you think transformation means?

- What is required for something to transform into something else?

- How long does transformation take?

Low-Energy Option — *Who's Who?*

[Before starting: In advance of your gathering, tell the students to bring two printed pictures of themselves: one as a baby, and one present-day picture. Attach the baby pictures to one piece of posterboard, placing a number beside each picture. Attach the present-day pictures to a different piece of posterboard, writing the name of the person below the picture. As the students arrive, give each person a piece of paper and a writing utensil.]

Say something like: While we are waiting on everyone to arrive, please look over these baby pictures. Once everyone is here, you will have two minutes to write down who you think each baby is. Please do not tell others which baby picture is yours.

[Once everyone has arrived . . .]

Say: Now you have two minutes to guess who each baby is. Write down the name of the person whom you think corresponds to the baby-picture number. You will get one point for each match you get correct. The person with the most number of points will win a Baby Ruth candy bar.

[After two minutes . . .]

Say: Everyone, write your names on your paper, then trade papers with the person sitting next to you.

Say: Please write the correct name next to the matching number on the paper of your neighbor before handing it back to them. If they have the correct name already, give them a smiley face.

Say: As I call out your baby-picture number, please come move your present-day picture beside your baby picture.

[Progress through the baby-picture numbers, until all present-day pictures are next to baby pictures.]

Ask:

- What kinds of physical changes are most common in growing from a baby to a teenager?

- What traits typically stay with us as we grow older?

- How do our relationships change as we grow older?

- What feelings are associated with changing into a different person?

Say something like: You are experiencing a lot of change right now, some changes more obvious than others. When we are talking about the change that God calls us to, we use the term *transformation*. It is an ongoing theme throughout Scripture. Some transformations seem instantaneous; some seem to take a long time, just like a tadpole's transformation happens faster than a caterpillar's. For more on what transformation means and why we are talking about it, let's watch this short video.

[Play Video 1.]

Explore (15 minutes)

Say something like: Today we are going to focus on transformation and the process of change that God is doing in each of us to help us become more like Christ. In your Student Guide, you will find a Scripture passage from Philippians 1:3-11 written for you and instructions with what to do as you read the passage. Please open your Student Guides and follow the instructions there.

[The students will read Philippians 1:3-11 and underline words that indicate forward progression or change in the subject.]

[After allowing the students four minutes to complete the activity...]

Say something like: Relationships are a very important part of going through transformation. We know from Acts 16 that Paul had a deep relationship with a group of people from Philippi whom he helped lead through a conversion to Christianity. His letter to the church that resulted from this transformation is the book of the Bible we call Philippians, one of the first churches he began in Europe.

Say: It is believed that when Paul was writing this letter to the Philippian church, he was being held prisoner in Rome. He had hoped to be able to return to Philippi to be with his church again, but was unavoidably detained.

Ask:

- When you receive a message of encouragement, how does it make you feel? Why?

- Can I have a volunteer read verses 3-6 from your Student Guide? Why would it be important for Paul to start a letter with such encouragement?

- If your pastor was to write a letter like this to you, how would that make you feel?

Say something like: You may or may not remember that Paul had his own very powerful transformation on a journey to Damascus. Through a whole series of events, which you can read more about in Acts 9, Paul was blinded for three days, then had his sight restored. As a result, he came to believe that Jesus was the Messiah. Paul knows that transformation can sometimes be painful, confusing, or scary. He also knows that communicating with God through it all is key. That communication most often, for us, takes the form of prayer. And so, Paul makes sure that his friends in Philippi struggling through their own transformation know that he's praying for them and that God will not leave them, though times are difficult.

Ask:

- If you ever had someone say to you, "I am praying for you," what kind of difference did that make in your life?

- What is the difference between Paul saying, "I am praying that you will do these things," and "I think you really need to be doing better at these things"?

- What do you think the role of prayer is in a person becoming more like Christ?

- How does the support of fellow believers impact the development of a person's relationship with Christ?

- How could being in relationship with people who have been transformed by God help shape your own transformation?

Reflect (5 minutes)

Say something like: Each person's journey with God is unique and, because of that, it is important for you to have a time to consider where you are individually on your journey. Please turn to the Reflect section of your Student Guide and follow the instructions listed.

I'm sure about this: the one who started a good work in you will stay with you to complete the job by the day of Christ Jesus (Philippians 1:6).

Ask: Can you think of ways God has worked in other people to impact your life? List them in your Student Guide.

Ask: What "good work" did God start because of you?

Ask: What work do you think God has for you to do in the next few months?

Ask: Is there something you've thought about doing for God, but never actually did? What has stopped you from getting started? What do you need to take the first step?

Create (10 minutes)

Relationship and Transformation

Say something like: While doing the work God has created you to do is a personal and unique task, you cannot do it alone. Most significant transformation requires some kind of outside help and encouragement to motivate you to change. Over the next few weeks, it will be important for us, as a group, to be there for one another and support one another as God continues to make you into Christ's image.

Say: Please form groups of three amongst yourselves. In your groups, come up with at least three encouraging statements you could share with other members of the group to help them when transformation gets hard or when they feel stuck.

Say: Then, either take or find pictures illustrating those encouraging statements. Each group will be asked to share their encouragement statements and pictures. You have five minutes. Please begin.

[After groups have shared all three of their encouragement statements and pictures . . .]

Ask:

- Why might it be dangerous to compare your transformation or your walk with Christ to someone else's?

- Do you think you have a responsibility to become involved with someone else's personal relationship with God? If yes, how do you do that? If no, why not?

- How can God use the painful experiences we go through to make us more like Christ?

- How would your life be different if, each morning when you woke up, you made a promise to yourself and God that "Today, I'm going to do one thing that makes me more like Christ"?

Next (3 minutes)

Decide What Really Matters

[Invite the students to turn in their Student Guides and review the Next section before closing in prayer.]

I pray this so that you will be able to decide what really matters and so you will be sincere and blameless on the day of Christ. I pray that you will then be filled with the fruit of righteousness, which comes from Jesus Christ, in order to give glory and praise to God (Philippians 1:10-11).

Say: This week, every morning when you're brushing your teeth, think of one thing you will do that will reflect Christ's image. Write it down in your Student Guide:

Day 1 —

Day 2 —

Day 3 —

Day 4 —

Day 5 —

Day 6 —

Say: Using one of the encouragement statements or pictures from today's session, send someone not in this study a Snapchat, direct message, text, email, or letter to encourage them in their faith journey.

Prayer

Ask for a volunteer to lead the closing prayer.

Leader: God, help our love and appreciation of others grow deeper as we walk closer with Christ.

People: God, help us decide what really matters.

Leader: God, erase all that separates us from you, and give us hearts full of sincere gratitude.

People: God, fill us with the Holy Spirit to live like Jesus and be servants for his name.

All: We ask all these things so that we can give you glory and praise.

2 The Faith Given to You

Summary

This lesson will help your students think more deeply about who has influenced their faith and whose faith they influence. We do not come to faith on our own; we have others who teach us about God and show us what it means to live out our faith. Having faith in God is a personal commitment that requires every individual to make decisions about what they will believe and how they will live out that belief.

Overview

- **Connect** though activities that get students thinking about what Christians do.

- **Explore** the use of metaphor as a way to make talking about faith more approachable.

- **Reflect** individually on core beliefs and the role tradition plays in faith development.

- **Create** a blueprint of your faith, considering who helped build the different parts of your faith.

- **Next,** become the builder and determine who God is calling you to help build up.

Anchor Point

1 Corinthians 3:5-6—After all, what is Apollos? What is Paul? They are servants who helped you to believe. Each one had a role given to them by the Lord: I planted, Apollos watered, but God made it grow.

16

Supplies

- "Christians Do" index cards

- Student Guides

- Pens/pencils

Parent Email

This week your student will be thinking about where their faith comes from, who has influenced their faith, and whose faith they influence. We encourage you to read 1 Corinthians 3:4-11 to be in conversation with your student this week about their journey.

We do not come to faith on our own; we have others who teach us about God and show us what it means to live out our faith. Research has shown that parents or caregivers are the most influential people in the development of the faith of adolescents. Hearing your faith journey will make your student more comfortable sharing stories about their own.

Share stories with your student about:

- someone who has shaped your faith

- a time you had the opportunity to shape someone else's faith

- how having a child(ren) has shaped your faith. Be sure to use an example of how the child in this study has impacted your faith.

Leader Notes

Remember that not all students will be at the same place in their faith journey or have had access to a consistent faith community. Therefore, when discussing who has been influential in their faith development, it will be crucial for you to not overemphasize the quantity of faithful people in their lives, but rather the quality of those who have faithfully supported the student.

Theology and Commentary

Because God is triunity—Father, Son, and Holy Spirit—God's design is for faith formation to happen in community. Not only are we developing a relationship with the Triune God—Father, Son, and Holy Spirit—but we do so alongside others in the church. Growing to love God more deeply depends on our interactions with others.

Jesus grew up in a tradition that highly valued teaching children the tenants of the faith. This command from God in Deuteronomy 11:18-20 would have shaped how Jesus and the disciples were raised:

Place these words I'm speaking on your heart and in your very being. Tie them on your hand as a sign. They should be on your forehead as a symbol. Teach them to your children, by talking about them when you are sitting around your house and when you are out and about, when you are lying down and when you are getting up. Write them on your house's doorframes and on your city's gates.

The passing along of the faith from one generation to the next is a cornerstone of Jewish tradition. The faith given to you was not just for you, but for those who came after you. However, Jesus' resurrection modifies that tradition and challenges his followers to not only share the faith with the family, but to "Go into the whole *world* and proclaim the good news to every creature" (Mark 16:15, emphasis added). The faith given to you is no longer just from your biological family, but from the Son of God.

Throughout his epistles, Paul is constantly encouraging new followers of Christ to support one another, teach one another, and learn from one another. The theme of unity is particularly evident in his first letter to the Corinthian church. This new community of predominately wealthy Gentile converts is having a difficult time staying civil (1 Corinthians 3:3). In the following section, 3:4-7, Paul establishes the necessity of teamwork and the centrality of God.

Paul notes that he and Apollos are after the same goal, with different means of execution. Their work as a team is to bring others closer to God. Neither can accomplish that goal alone because each has his own role to play. The team has no control over how their work will grow. Paul uses the metaphor of planting, growing, and building to further enlighten the Corinthians on their own plight. The metaphors push the readers of the letter to come to grips with how faith interconnects each participant in the community with one another and with God.

When the community of believers are all working together to nurture one another's faith, the family of faith is invigorated to expand into an open-source community that shares the gospel freely to all people.

Open-source disciple-making means there will be many people in the community who contribute to our understanding of who God is and how we relate to God. Some of them will be biological family members; some of them will be members of the Christian family; and even others will be members of a different faith tradition or no faith at all. In accepting our commission, we stand on the foundation laid by Jesus Christ, through the lives of the generations of disciples who came before us.

Leader Reflection

Read 1 Corinthians 3:4-11 and John 15:1-17.

Have you ever been responsible for keeping a plant alive? It seems to be an easy enough task: regular water, adequate sunlight, and enough room for roots to grow. Yet for some reason, it's incredibly easy to forget and, all of a sudden, your plant has shriveled up and died.

Faith is the same way. It seems to be an easy enough task to grow your faith: regular Scripture reading, a good deal of prayer, and loving the community around you. But all too often, we are seeing the faith of our young people shrivel and die. You have been tasked to help grow the faith of the young people in your care. However, if your faith is parched, you will have very little to pour into your students. Allow yourself a few moments to take stock of your spiritual growth practices. Are you spending adequate time in prayer? How often are you reading God's Word? How have you been in service to others?

If you find you are not satisfied with the answers to these questions, then what are the barriers preventing you to have the water, sunlight, or room you need to grow? What can you do or who can you enlist to help you overcome these barriers?

In preparation for leading this lesson, complete the Create and Next activities from the Student Book. Sharing your experiences will encourage the students to share their own.

Be in prayer for your students and your preparation:

- Ask God to help you be the water your students need or to be able to get your students to the nourishment they need.

- Thank God for the many people in your life who have helped you have the faith you have today, and for the people who continue to push you to grow further.

Connect (8 minutes)

High-Energy Option—*Never Have I Ever*

[Before the lesson, create a deck of "Christians Do" index cards. On each card, write one activity associated with being a Christian. Try to come up with at least two cards for every student in your group. Some examples may include: read the entire Bible, sing in a church choir or praise band, go on a mission trip, set up chairs in the fellowship hall, be a sheep in the Christmas pageant, fall asleep during the pastor's sermon, attend a Bible study. Try to think of a few activities all your students would have done, as well as some only a few have done. Arrange the chairs in the room into a circle, with one less chair than the number of students you have. Spread the deck of cards out, words down, on the floor and offer the following instructions.]

Say: I need one volunteer to start our game. You will pick up a card off the floor and say, "Never have I ever . . . ," then finish the sentence with what is written on the card. Those sitting in the circle, if you have done the activity read from the card, you must get out of your seat and find another seat before everyone else, including the person who just read the card. The person left without a seat will then pick up a card off the floor and read another "Christians Do" statement. We will keep going until all the cards have been read.

[Play the game until all the cards have been read. Arrange all the cards, "Christians Do" statements facing up, on the floor in the middle of the circle.]

Ask:

- Looking at these "Christians Do" statements, which ones seem to cause Christians to judge one another the most? Why do you think we do that?

- How do you tell the difference between how God wants you to grow your faith and how others think you should grow your faith?

- Imagine you are new to the Christian faith. What would you feel looking at this deck of cards?

- How do we help non-Christians or new Christians see the Christian faith as more than a "to-do list"?

Low-Energy Option — *What Is Necessary?*

[Before the lesson, create a deck of "Christians Do" index cards. On each card, write one activity associated with being a Christian. Try to come up with at least two cards for every student in your group. Examples are listed in the instructions for the High-Energy activity. Try to think of a few activities all your students would have done, as well as some only a few have done. Hand at least one card to each student as they arrive. Once everyone is there and seated, offer the following instructions.]

Say: I am going to ask one person at a time to read the "to-do" statement on your index card. Then, as a group, we will decide if this is an activity that is necessary, optional, or not necessary to do to be a Christian. The reader of the card will then place the necessary card here *(indicate a place to put the card)*, optional card here, and not-necessary card here. Once all the cards have been read, we will go through each category and see if we need to make any changes.

[Once all the cards have been read, go through each category starting with the not-necessary cards, and discuss why they are there and if there are any that need to be moved.]

Ask:

- Looking at these "Christians Do" statements, which ones seem to cause Christians to judge one another the most? Why do you think we do that?

- How do you tell the difference between how God wants you to grow your faith and how others think you should grow your faith?

- Imagine you are new to the Christian faith. What would you feel looking at this deck of cards?

- How do we help non-Christians or new Christians see the Christian faith as more than a "to-do list"?

Say something like: Sometimes we can feel like there's a lot of pressure on us to behave correctly or check the right "Christians Do" boxes. We also have the tendency to judge our fellow believers who we think aren't checking the right boxes. People have lots of opinions on what you should believe and how you should practice your faith. There are some basic practices that Christians should be involved in, not because of others' perceptions or guilt for doing it, but for the joy of being with God. Ultimately, what you do in service to God and to grow your faith will be your decision. Your faith is your own, and you will do what you do and live as you think God is calling you to live.

Explore (15 minutes)

[Ask for two volunteers to read aloud the Scripture printed in the Explore section of the Student Guide.]

Reader 1: 1 Corinthians 3:4-8, and Reader 2: 1 Corinthians 3:9-11

After the reading, **ask the entire group:**

- Which do you think is a better metaphor for growing your faith—being a plant in God's field or building God's building? Why?

Say something like: Metaphor is a literary style used often throughout Scripture, and Jesus was the master of metaphor. A few of Jesus' greatest hits include this from John 3:19: "The light came into the world, and people loved darkness more than the light, for their actions are evil." Another from John 10:11: "I am the good shepherd. The good shepherd lays down his life for the sheep."

Say: The use of metaphor in Scripture is helpful because it allows people to understand faith, even if they don't know the language of the faith tradition. If you were to tell some of your friends that Jesus is the redeemer of all humankind and cleanses them of their iniquity, they would look at you like you were speaking another language. And in a way, you are. But if you were to say Jesus is like a great rainstorm in the middle of a drought; he brings dead grass back to life and washes away the dust that covers everything: this is a concept they can understand.

Say: Metaphors provide the opportunity for the Holy Spirit to connect with each person's heart and give understanding.

Say: Without trying to sound like your English teacher, it's important to remember that a simile is a metaphor that uses *like* or *as* to make a comparison, or to make a distinction more prominent. It's often easier for us to draw comparisons through simile.

Say: Since metaphors can be so powerful in helping us understand our faith, you are going to spend a few minutes working in groups to create some modern-day metaphors. If your group would prefer to illustrate a simile instead of writing in metaphor, that is an option your whole group can decide on.

Make Your Own Metaphor

[Separate the group into smaller groups of two or three, depending on your size and space. Give each group about five minutes to work together. Be sure to be a part of each group discussion to offer help or further explanation. Once groups have had enough time to develop their metaphor, ask each group to share their metaphors with the entire group.]

Reflect (3 minutes)

Say something like: Each person's journey with God is unique and, because of that, it is important for you to have a time to consider where you are individually on your journey. Please turn to the Reflect section of your Student Guide and follow the prompts listed.

Say: List three core beliefs you have about Jesus.

Ask: What is something you've been taught that you are not sure you believe?

Ask: What is one practice of the church you would like to change? Why and how?

Say something like: For those who feel comfortable, I would like to offer the opportunity to share your core beliefs about Jesus.

[Allow time for the students to share as they are comfortable.]

Say: Thank you for being willing to share those personal insights with the group. I appreciate your honesty and openness.

Say: Videos can be another artistic way in which we can express metaphors. We're going to watch a short video now that illustrates what we mean by forming or shaping your own faith.

[Play Video 2.]

Create (10 minutes)

Say something like: Metaphors are useless unless you think through how exactly they apply to your life. You are going to have some time now, individually, to think through the forming of your faith as a house blueprint.

Say: In your Student Guide, you will find a cross-section sketch of a house, with parts of the house listed. Take some time now, following the prompts listed, to think about who has been a construction worker in building your faith.

Building Your Faith

[Before gathering, complete this activity for yourself.]

[Allow five minutes for the students to complete the activity on their own. Once everyone is done . . .]

Ask:

- As you look at the people who have been a part of growing your faith, is there anything all these people have in common? If so, what is it?

- What about who they are or what they did makes them stand out to you?

- Are there any behaviors or habits these people have that you would like to copy? How do you think that would help your own faith?

- Can you think of someone who has helped grow your faith because of a negative experience you had with them? What did they help you learn?

Say something like: Growing our faith is not always about positive, uplifting encounters with wonderful, loving people. The truth is that we experience negative, heartbreaking, ugly things that could turn us away from God. However, one of our core beliefs is that God can redeem even the worst experiences of our lives to bring about a richer and more beautiful faith, if we allow it. To push the metaphor a little more, God can help us patch up the hole in the drywall, if we just ask for the help.

Next (3 minutes)

Who Are You Building Up?

[Before starting, complete this activity for yourself.]

Say: In the passage we read earlier from 1 Corinthians, Paul says, "Each person needs to pay attention to the way they build on it" (3:10). This implies that he expects each person to be responsible for helping to build up the faith of others. Following the instructions in your Student Guide in the Next section, spend three minutes thinking about how YOU could be a construction worker in building someone else's faith.

Say: In the circle, write one way you can help someone grow or build their faith *(how you can be a farmer or construction worker)*.

Say: At the end of the arrows, write the names of three people you think God is calling you to help.

Say something like: Today we have considered many different ways in which our faith has been formed. There have been important people who have helped get us to where we are in our journey with God right now. As we continue our faith journey in this group, you will play a role in the faith of every member of this group. Your opinions, questions, and reflections will help build the faith of this community. That is how we will learn who God is calling us to be: a planter, a waterer, or a builder.

Prayer

[Close in a time of prayer using the following petitions.]

Say: I am going to lead us in closing prayer. I will begin the prayer, and then ask you to say aloud the name of someone who fits that petition. Let us pray:

Creator God, thank you for all the wonderful people who have helped us along our faith journey. We want to especially thank you for the people who have taught us the most about following you. *(Allow time of silence for students to share names.)*

Redeeming Jesus, we are so grateful for the love you freely give us all the time. We want to say thanks for the people who have shown us what it means to love like you. *(Allow time of silence for students to share names.)*

Supporting Spirit, we know we could not do this without your help and guidance. We want to ask your help to build the faith of our friends. *(Allow time of silence for students to share names.)*

God, we are excited to be on this journey with you. Thanks for sticking with us and helping us through. Help us to see your direction as we go through this week. In the name of Jesus Christ, we pray. Amen.

3 *Life in Christ*

Summary

The questions your students have been considering this week are "Who do you resemble?" and "How is your life a reflection of God?" This lesson will challenge students to consider the many characteristics of God and how they embody those to be a reflection of the divine image.

Overview

- **Connect** through activities to get students focused on character traits or the fruit of the Spirit in the group.

- **Explore** the characteristics of God and how we embody the divine image.

- **Reflect** on how anti-fruits of the Spirit can impact our relationship with God.

- **Create** a church event celebrating and using every fruit of the Spirit.

- **Next,** strengthen your relationship with God through focusing on the fruit of the Spirit.

Anchor Point

Galatians 5:22-23—But the fruit of the Spirit is love, joy, peace, patience, kindness, goodness, faithfulness, gentleness, and self-control. There is no law against things like this.

Supplies

- High-Energy Supplies: autographed photograph of someone from your church whom all the students would recognize (pastor, youth leader, parent), index card with the name of the person from the photograph written on it (Note—If you would like to play the High-Energy game multiple times, multiple pictures and index cards will be necessary.)

- Low-Energy Supplies: Student Guides, nine components of the fruit of the Spirit listed individually on sheets of paper (see Anchor Point Scripture); sticky notes—red/pink, green, and yellow; three sheets of blank notebook paper (one piece for each squad)

- Three sheets of poster paper (11-by-17 if possible), one piece for each squad

- Student Guides

- Bibles or Bible app

- Pens/pencils

Parent Email

We are continuing in our faith discovery this week to begin considering what a life in Christ looks like. Through spiritual disciplines and our group discussion, we will focus on the many characteristics of God and how to embody those to be a reflection of the divine image.

During our group time together, we will be spending time in Galatians 5:22-26, a passage in which Paul identifies the fruit of the Spirit. We encourage you to have some conversation with your student and practice the fruit of the Spirit, which encompasses: love, joy, peace, patience, kindness, goodness, faithfulness, gentleness, and self-control.

Leader Notes

Trying to act like someone else or appear to be like another person is going to be a familiar concept to many of your students. The desire to belong is strong in adolescents. This should be an opportunity for you to highlight the positive aspects of being part of the family of God.

Our desire to be like Christ, to embody the characteristics of God, is not a result of something wrong with us, but a desire to strengthen our relationship with God. Please be conscious that most students will not consider themselves possessing all or maybe any of the components of the fruit of the Spirit. Encourage them that part of the faith journey is opening themselves to the opportunities for the Spirit to help them grow, and something they will be continually working toward.

Theology and Commentary

There are many different avenues to explore when we are learning to live a life in Christ. Jesus taught parables to help us understand what it meant to follow him. All of the epistles at some point or another explain how we are to be imitators of God (Ephesians 5:1-2). With so many avenues out there, it can become an overwhelming endeavor to figure out what it means to live a life in Christ.

Paul saw this in the Galatian church. In Chapter 5, he gives them a long list of behaviors and attitudes that are not fitting for disciples of Christ (Galatians 5:16-21). Who hasn't wanted to give a teenager a list of things not to do and say, "Stay away from this and you'll turn out all right, kid"? However, as the authors of *Growing Young* point out, "Too many restrictions without hopeful yeses create more than boundaries; they create identity, belonging, and purpose dead ends. . . . The no's declare a boundary, but they don't provide a hopeful way forward toward and new vision for living."[1]

Paul's list doesn't end with the 17 no's. He understands that these people need a hopeful way forward. In a turnaround, Paul lists only nine ways of behaving that are indicative of followers of Christ. And he qualifies these behaviors not as fruits of individual action, but as the fruit of the Spirit.

These are behaviors that come from the Holy Spirit, not from the individual—ways of living that are a result of being connected with God. For the first two-thirds of this chapter, Paul is drawing our attention to how our selfishness disconnects us from God. Then he quite simply says if you put aside your selfishness, then the Holy Spirit can do these amazing things through you.

---

1 Kara Powell, Jake Mulder, and Brad Griffin, *Growing Young: Six Essential Strategies to Help Young People Discover and Love Your Church* (Baker Books: Grand Rapids, 2016), 142.

Leader Reflection

Read Galatians 5:1-26.

An adult Sunday school class kept an empty coffee can on a table in their classroom. Each Sunday, members of the class would drop loose change and small bills into the coffee can. The money collected was sent to a child they supported in a different country. The can rarely had more than $15.00 in it.

One Sunday, the class leader was absent and the money was not collected after class. The following Sunday, the money was gone. After checking around, it was discovered that no one from the class or the church leadership had collected the money. Class members were angry. Who would steal from a Sunday school class, an orphan? How horrible it is that even our church classrooms are not safe from thieves!

Betty didn't join those sentiments. She, in her quiet, still-powerful voice, said, "Well, whoever took the money must have really needed it." And in her assertion that their money went to someone who really needed it, even if it was stolen, Betty embodied the fruit of the Spirit. In her refusal to condemn this unknown thief, she showed love, kindness, goodness, and faithfulness. In her prophetic voice to her brothers and sisters in Christ, she showed joy, peace, patience, gentleness, and self-control. This is what it means to live by the fruit of the Spirit: a life in Christ.

Consider who has shown you the fruit of the Spirit.

Has there been a time when you were an angered class member, instead of a graceful Betty?

What will you need to do to live with the fruit of the Spirit more instinctually?

Be in prayer for your students and your preparation.

Ask for the chance to live the fruit of the Spirit.

Connect (6 minutes)

High-Energy Option—*Person Pictionary*

Form two equal teams.

Give these instructions: Each team will need to designate one person on their team to be the illustrator. I will give the illustrator from Group A a photograph of someone from our church everyone knows.

Say: I will give the illustrator from Group B the name of the person in the photograph given to Group A. This name will be written on an index card.

Say: Both groups will be trying to identify the same person. Both illustrators will be simultaneously drawing pictures to lead his or her team to guess who this person is. The sketches cannot contain letters or numbers.

Say: Once the illustrators have been given their person, and I make sure they know who that person is, I will give them five seconds before they must begin to sketch.

Say: After the five seconds are up, I will set a timer to one minute, and the illustrators must sketch their clues.

Say: If no one guesses the person after one minute, a new illustrator must be chosen, a new timer will be set for thirty seconds, and teams will continue to guess. Previous illustrators will not be allowed to guess, but must remain quiet until the game is completed.

Say: The first team to guess the person correctly wins the autographed photograph, and bragging rights.

Following the game, **say:**

- Compare how the illustrators chose to depict the person.

- Did getting two different types of clues impact the depiction? If so, how?

- What was the final part of the drawing that made you realize who they were depicting?

Low-Energy Option—*Red Light, Yellow Light, Green Light*[2]

[Before the students arrive: List the nine components of the fruit of the Spirit on pieces of paper. Post these nine pieces of paper on the walls around the room.]

Give these instructions: In your Student Guide in the Connect section, you will find a list of the fruit of the Spirit. Review this list. Next to each fruit of the Spirit, write the word "Red," "Yellow," or "Green" that corresponds to your confidence in having that fruit of the Spirit. The colors and confidence levels are noted in your Student Guide. *[Allow time for writing.]*

Give these instructions: Everyone at one time is going to come and take the number of and color of sticky notes to correspond with what you wrote in your guide. Take as many red, yellow, and green sticky notes as you need and post your answers on the fruit of the Spirit papers around the room. For example, if you wrote GREEN beside LOVE in your Student Guide, then you would put a green sticky note on the LOVE paper. *[Allow time to complete activity.]*

Say something like: Let's take a look at how the fruit of the Spirit is represented in our group. I am not going to ask who put what colors where because that's not particularly important at this point. What is important is that we see where we have an abundance of fruit and where we have a lack of fruit.

Ask: If all of the components of the fruit of the Spirit are not represented, what does that tell us about how open we are to God?

Ask: How do you think presence of the fruit of the Spirit might impact our outreach and the perceptions non-Christians have of our church?

---

2 Ibid, 222.

Affirm Leader Guide

Explore (17 minutes)

Look Around

[Form three teams of roughly an equal number of students. Then assign each team a person of the Trinity (God, Jesus, Holy Spirit). This will be their squad for the rest of the session.]

Give these instructions: In your Student Guide, you will find Scripture passages and instructions listed for each squad. Each of you are trying to come up with character traits for your member of the Trinity based on what you can find in the Scripture passages. You will have ten minutes to find and write down the character traits that make up your person. If you think of other passages that describe the character of your person, please feel free to add those, but be ready to read your examples from Scripture! After ten minutes, I'll take your paper, post it here, and we'll compare.

[After giving time for students to look through their passages . . .]

Say something like: Before we compare what you found in your Scripture passages, I just want to remind you that this is not everything the Bible has to say about God, Jesus, or the Holy Spirit. Part of growing as a disciple is continuing to read and examine Scripture to learn more about the vast character of God the Father, Son, and Holy Spirit.

Say: As a step in that direction, let's take a few minutes now to compare these characteristics you have found in your quick ten-minute search. I'll ask each group to bring up your list, and then we'll circle the characteristics that all three members of the Trinity have in common.

Say something like: There is no way we could understand all there is to know about God in this lifetime. Even if we had endless time and resources, there are characteristics of God that are just beyond our understanding. But we can connect with God on several levels because we are part of God's creation and, therefore, part of God. That's where these characteristics come in.

Say: I need two volunteers to read a couple different Scripture passages, two verses each. You'll find them printed in your Student Guide.

Volunteer 1 reads Genesis 1:26-27.

Say something like: If we are made in the divine image of God, then we should have all the same characteristics of God that we've listed on these sheets. Luckily for us, quite a while back, somebody thought it would be a good idea to boil down these characteristics into a list that's more manageable. Paul decided to call them the fruit of the Spirit. Let's be reminded of what they are now.

Volunteer 2 reads Galatians 5:22-23.

[Play Video 3.]

Following the video, **ask:**

- What connections do you see between character traits of God and the fruit of the Spirit?

- How can the fruit of the Spirit help us better understand God and improve our relationship with God?

- If the fruit of the Spirit isn't something we do but something God does in us, how do we get God to do it?

- How does the fruit of the Spirit allow humanity to reflect the divine image?

- What happens when we begin to resemble God?

Reflect (3 minutes)

Say something like: Each person's journey with God is unique, and because of that, it is important for you to have time to consider where you are individually on your journey. Please turn to the Reflect section of your Student Guide and follow the instructions listed.

Galatians 5:25-26: If we live by the Spirit, let's follow the Spirit. Let's not become arrogant, make each other angry, or be jealous of each other.

Say: List the components of the fruit of the Spirit. Beside each, write an antonym *(or opposite)* to that word *(example, Peace/Anxiety)*.

Ask: Which of these anti-fruit most separates you from God?

Ask: How is your anti-fruit impacting your resemblance of God?

Ask: How can arrogance, anger, or jealousy turn the fruit of the Spirit into an anti-fruit?

Create (15 minutes)

Fruit-of-the-Spirit Church Event

Say something like: If the fruit of the Spirit helps us see God in individuals, then could a church have the fruit of the Spirit? What would a CHURCH full of people with the fruit of the Spirit look like?

Say: I am going to ask you to get back in the same squads you were in earlier. As a group, you are going to plan a mock church event. This mock event should allow all participants to experience all the components of the fruit of the Spirit.

Say: Here's what you need to decide:

• Who's invited?

• What will the invited do?

• What will the people hosting do? What are their responsibilities?

• What conflicts may arise and how will they be handled?

• How will each of the parts of the fruit of the Spirit be exhibited?

Say: You will need to have one person from your group record the group's answers in their Student Guide.

Say: Once you have an idea of what you want to do, your group will create a flyer, using your answers to these questions, to advertise your church event. I will give each group a piece of poster paper for you to present to the group.

Say: After ten minutes, I'm going to ask each group to share their flyers for their fruit-of-the-Spirit mock church event.

[Allow time for sharing.]

[Once all groups have shared . . .]

Ask:

- How would ministry at this church change if every church leader had to make sure that every church ministry exhibited the fruit of the Spirit?

- What is the responsibility of the community of believers to support one another in walking with Christ?

- What happens when the church begins to resemble God?

- How can you respectfully remind someone of their commitment to growing more like Christ?

Next (3 minutes)

[Invite the students to turn in their Student Guides and review the Next section before closing in prayer.]

Say: Think of someone whom you believe shows the fruit of the Spirit often. Send them a text/note thanking them for their example. Ask them to pray for you so you can do better showing others the fruit of the Spirit.

Prayer

God, we thank you for the way you live in us. We are humbled when we remember that you made us in YOUR image. We ask that you strengthen us to reflect you in this world. Help us to live by the fruit of your Spirit. In our hearts now, we ask you to help each of us with one fruit specifically.

[Allow a moment for personal prayer.]

Give us the courage to live by love, joy, peace, patience, kindness, goodness, faithfulness, gentleness, and self-control.

We pray in the name of Jesus, through the power of the Holy Spirit, for your glory, God.

Amen.

4 Know What You Believe

Summary

Most teenagers will have someone in their circle of friends, relatives, or neighbors who does not believe that God matters. Part of growing in faith is being able to explain to others why God does matter. Of the many reasons why, the purpose of this lesson is to focus on why God's love matters most, and help students explore why God's love matters to them.

Overview

- **Connect** through a choice of activities that challenges the students to think about partnership and love.

- **Explore** the impact God's sacrificial love has on the world, our communities, and individuals.

- **Reflect** on what difference you have seen God make.

- **Create** annotated belief statements for a limited character world.

- **Next,** discover ways God shows us love each day.

Anchor Point

Ephesians 2:8-9 — You are saved by God's grace because of your faith. This salvation is God's gift. It's not something you possessed. It's not something you did that you can be proud of.

Supplies

- High-Energy Supplies: one coin (for flipping), two boxes, two shareable prizes, wrapping/newspaper, tape, gloves, blindfolds

- Low-Energy Supplies: hymnals, paper, internet-connected devices (optional)

- Red construction paper, scissors

- Student Guides

- Bibles or Bible app

- Pencils/pens

Parent Email

Your student is now halfway through a study exploring how they can live what they believe. Living your faith is based on the assumption that you believe God loves you and everyone around you. Sometimes this is a hard concept for adults to grasp, more difficult still for teenagers.

Pray for your student as they work through their faith practices this week and are challenged to think deeply about what it means that God loves them.

Talk with your student:

- Share an experience in your life when you were certain of God's love for you.

- Share a time in your life when you were uncertain of God's love for you, and what happened to change your fears.

- Share what having a child of your own has taught you about love.

Leader Notes

Lesson 4: Know What You Believe and Lesson 5: Know Why You Believe are two sides of the same coin. Topics that are covered in this lesson will be highly relevant to the topics that will be covered in the following lesson.

Many teens in our society live with the constant uncertainty of their worth to be loved by anyone. As you are covering these topics, please be alert to statements and reactions that may indicate a student is harming themselves or considering harming themselves. Drench conversations about self-worth in prayer, grace, and love.

Theology and Commentary

All of Ephesians 2 is a great pep talk for trusting in God's love for us. Scholars believe the letter to the Ephesians was not meant for just one church, as some of Paul's letters were. The lack of specificity allows a present-day reader to easily identify with its teachings. The theme of unity and wholeness that runs throughout the letter makes it approachable for adolescents looking for confirmation that they belong.

If Ephesians 2 gives us a clear, approachable, and hopeful understanding of how God has drawn us together as one family, then Revelation 21 paints for us a picture of what it is we are united for. Prophecy is often not so clear and approachable. But the prophetic image depicted in the first few verses of Revelation 21 offers us a glimpse of the world we long to have: a world without death, mourning, crying, or pain; a world surrounded by nothing but God's pure love. Putting scrolls, angels, and plagues aside, the concept of being surrounded by pure love is difficult enough to imagine. But this is what we have been promised, and this is what we are striving to achieve.

This is what we are meaning when we pray, "Thy kingdom come, thy will be done on earth as it is in heaven." This is the result of the unity of Ephesians and the promise of Revelation—that we work and pray for God's love to become so much a part of who we are and how we live that we actually create a community of pure love. God's presence in and through us changes how the world around us looks, feels, and operates. God has the ability to make all things new through each and every one of God's children, now and in the future generations.

Leader Reflection

Read Ephesians 2:4-9 and Revelation 21:1-5.

Do you believe Jesus Christ died for your sins? In certain circumstances or on certain occasions, this question may cause you to roll your eyes, get huffy, or even close and lock the front door without a backward glance. When asked by a stranger, this question can come across intrusive or worse, judgmental. But truly, this is a question we should constantly be asking ourselves: Do I truly believe God loves ME enough to die for all the ways I mess up every day?

The certainty of God's love, as demonstrated in the life, death, and resurrection of Jesus, is a cornerstone of the Christian faith (Ephesians 2:20). However, there are relationships in our lives, people in our society, and global catastrophes that can cause us to doubt that love. The passage from Ephesians reminds us, "You are saved by God's grace! . . . God did this to show future generations the greatness of his grace by the goodness that God has shown us in Christ Jesus" (2:5, 7). You are saved by God's grace, in relationship with Jesus Christ, so you can explain what salvation means to the generation gathering with you each week.

Your students have wondered or will wonder if Jesus really died for them. You are working together to build a faith that is strong enough to hold up under that kind of scrutiny and insecurity. You won't be able to convince your students of God's love unless:

1) you know God loves you without exception

2) you see why God loves them for who they are

3) you open their eyes to God's love all around them

Be in prayer for your students and your preparation:

- Thank God for the gracious gift of your salvation.

- Ask God to help you to communicate what you believe in a way that demonstrates love and grace.

- Listen for God's direction to which of your students needs to be reassured of God's love for him/her.

- Ask God for the grace to be an instrument of love and forgiveness.

Connect (5 minutes)

High-Energy Option—*Somebody with You*

[In preparation for the lesson, put something fun but shareable inside two boxes. Tape both boxes closed and double-wrap them in newspaper. Make sure to use too much tape. The items inside the box can be something like a bag of candy, roll of coins, and so forth.]

After the students have gathered, give these instructions.

Say: I need three volunteers to play a game together. There will be a prize for the winners at the end.

Say: I need two of you to volunteer to be blindfolded and wear these gloves.

[Once you have two volunteers, blindfold them and put gloves on them (vinyl gloves, snow gloves, mittens).]

After the two students are blindfolded and gloved, **say:** I am going to hand each of you a box. The box is double-wrapped in paper and taped overly well. Inside the box is a prize that you will get to have if you are the first person to get your box open.

Ask the third volunteer: *(Name),* I am going to flip a coin. If it lands on heads, you're with *(name one student).* If it lands on tails, you are with *(name other student).* Now, you can help your partner in any way you would like to get the box open, EXCEPT you cannot touch the box yourself. You can give encouragement, instructions, reports on how the other blindfolded person is doing, but you cannot under any circumstances touch the box. Your blindfolded partner can choose to accept your help or not, and in the end, if he/she wins, choose to share the prize with you or not.

Say: Everyone understand the rules? Everyone ready?

Say: Let crazy opening begin!

After the game is completed, **ask:**

- How was the game different for the person who did it on their own versus the person who had a partner?

- Who was more efficient in the problem-solving? Why?

- Did it seem fair that one person had support and the other did not? Why was it fair or not fair?

- How does having a partner make problems more manageable?

- How does knowing you have support impact the belief that you will succeed?

Say: Today we are going to be talking about why God matters and how God impacts our lives. God is not some distant deity keeping score of our rights and wrongs. God is involved in our everyday lives and offers us support for each decision we have to make. God makes a difference in our daily lives through constant love and grace.

Low-Energy Option—*Love Lyrics*

Once students have gathered, **say:** I am going to ask all of you to find a partner or make a group of three if you need to. Try to have at least one person in each group with a device that can connect to the internet. If there are not enough smartphones or tablets for one per group, we'll have to go "old school" and just use hymnals and your brains.

[Allow time for pairing.]

Say: Now that everyone has a partner or group, I'm going to give each group a number. Your group will have two minutes to think of or find as many lyrics as you can that relate to love. Write down all the lyrics you come up with on a piece of paper. The lyrics can be secular or religious. The lyrics do not have to contain the world "love," but must obviously be talking about love, loving, or being in love.

Say: There are hymnals on the table. If you all have access to a device connected to the internet, then everyone can use that to help resource lyrics as well. After the two minutes is up, we're going to have a "sing-off," but you don't have to sing.

Say: The person who has a birthday closest to today, their group gets to share their lyric first. They can sing or say it. Any group can jump in next with a lyric containing any of the words from the previously offered lyric, but it must still be related to love. One point is awarded to each group that successfully shares a lyric. Lyrics may not be repeated, but different lyrics from the same song are acceptable. Here's an example: *loving you is easy because you're beautiful; it's so easy to fall in love; you took the fall and thought of me above all.*

Say: An extra point will be awarded to a group that is able to put out a lyric that nobody can follow. They also get to start the next round.

Say: We will play until a group scores ten points. Your two minutes starts NOW!

[Allow two minutes for lyric searching and writing. During those two minutes, write the numbers of each group on a board or paper on the wall so that you can keep track of the score during the sing-off rounds.]

Ask: Whose birthday is closest to today? Ready? Give us the first lyric.

[Remember to give a point to each group that successfully shares a love lyric, and two points to the team that stumps all the other teams.]

Once a team reaches ten points, declare them the winner and then **ask the whole group:**

- What do lyrics about love have in common?

- How does music help us talk about love?

- How can music help to explain God's love to people who might not get it?

Say: Today we are going to be talking about why God matters and how God impacts our lives. God is not some distant deity keeping score of our rights and wrongs. God is involved in our everyday lives and loves us through each decision we have to make. God makes a difference in our daily lives through constant love and grace.

Explore (10 minutes)

Say something like: The primary belief that makes us Christians and distinct from other faiths is our belief that Jesus, being God's Son, sacrificed himself to free us from sin. We believe that this sacrifice was proof of God's unconditional love for us.

Say: The amount God loves you does not depend on you choosing church over sports or the Bible over PlayStation or Jesus over the latest YouTube celebrity. God loves you and sticks with you, no matter what choices you make. God loves you, even if you make poor choices or if you think you're not worth loving.

Say: God has done things in the past and will do things in the future to make sure you know that you are loved, valued, and a precious part of the family. We are now going to move into large groups to explore more about God's love for us.

[If you played "Love Lyrics" and made numbered teams, using the numbered teams as a reference, combine groups to form two larger groups. For example, groups 1–3 become Team Past, and groups 4–6 become Team Future. If you did not, evenly separate the students into two equal teams, designating one Team Past and the other Team Future.]

Say: Team Past, you are going to explore Ephesians 2:4-9, and Team Future, you are going to explore Revelation 21:1-5.

Say: You will find the passages in your Student Guide, as well as the questions you will need to answer together in your group.

Say: You will have five minutes to discuss these questions in your group. Be sure to write down some notes in your Student Guide about what you discussed.

Say: After five minutes, I'll ask for a volunteer from your group to read your Scripture passage and share the answers your group came up with to the discussion questions.

[Group discussion questions based on their reading:]

- How did God's actions impact the world?

- How did God's actions impact humanity?

- How will God's actions impact your life?

[After five minutes, or sooner if it seems the groups are done, . . .]

Say: I'm going to ask each group to read their passage and share their answers. Remember, both groups will be answering the same questions based on different Scripture passages, so it's OK if your answers are different.

[Allow time for sharing and discussion of the answers offered, as needed.]

Say: We have these two different passages, one about what God has done and one about what God will do. Based on both of these passages then . . .

- Why does God matter?

- What difference does God make?

- Why will your life be different because of God?

After a time of discussion, **say something like:** Part of the joy of being a child of God is being able to love like God. But you can't share God's love with others until you first understand how much God loves you. Understanding God's love for us opens us to love and be loved by others. God matters because God made you. Remember from last time, you are made in the divine image. And because you are made in the image of God, you are worthy of all of God's love and all the love of God's children.

Say: When God makes things new, God doesn't just change the world, God changes each and every individual in the world. Maybe God has already made something new in you.

[Play Video 4.]

Reflect (4 minutes)

Say something like: Each person's journey with God is unique and, because of that, it is important for you to have a time to consider where you are individually on your journey. Please turn to the Reflect section of your Student Guide and follow the instructions listed.

Ask: What difference has God made in your life?

Ask: How has God impacted the life of someone you know?

Say: Write about a time when you felt God didn't matter.

Say: Sketch a moment in your life when you knew God was close to you.

Create (12 minutes)

Say: It's time to write down what you believe. Not in a stone tablet, but in a tweet, a six-word memoir, or in 25 words or less. In your Student Guide, there are three categories for you to write down what you believe. Take two minutes to select a category and write what you believe in the style indicated. You will be asked to share your writing in a group that selected the same category as you.

[Circulate around the room while students are writing. If you notice that most students are choosing the same mode of communication, when everyone is done writing, have the students count off 1-2-3. The 1's will work on a tweet, 2's will work on six-word memoirs, and 3's will do 25 words or less. Otherwise, give the below instructions as written.]

Say: Everyone who chose to tweet what they believe about God, form one group. Those who wrote a six-word memoir, form another. And those who chose 25 words or less, form the final group.

Say: Take a moment to share your belief statement from your group. Once everyone has shared, as a group and using the same category, create a group statement of belief, drawing on the individual statements. Be prepared to share your group's statements with everyone.

[As the groups share, write down each category statement so that you can send them to students later in the week.]

After groups have shared, **ask:**

- Why is it important to be able to write down what you believe?

- What does it require for you to shorten your beliefs into so few words or characters?

- What are the positives and negatives of having to be concise with what you believe?

- What happens when we don't agree on what people should believe?

Next (2 minutes)

Say: We can struggle to believe God loves us at times because we do not pay attention to the ways God shares love with us each day.

[If time allows, ask each student to cut out a heart from construction paper and write their acts of love on their heart. Then, as they share their acts of love with one another, they can hang them on a wall in the room. If time is tight, follow the instructions below.]

Say: Turn in your Student Guide together to find instructions on what to do next.

Say: Another way we can recognize acts of love is by hearing what other people consider loving. I would like to ask if each of you would share one loving thing you've seen happen during our time together today. This way we can begin to understand the many ways we know God's love.

Prayer

[Please use the version of the Lord's Prayer that is most familiar to your students.]

Say something like: It's hard to find words to pray when we are not exactly sure what we want to say. So, today we are going to close by praying the Lord's Prayer. We are going to pray this because it's a prayer that requires us to recognize our sins and ask for forgiveness, as well as points out how God continues to take care of us. AND, it reminds us that it's not about us, but all about God. Let's pray:

Our father, who art in heaven,

hallowed be thy name.

Thy kingdom come,

thy will be done on earth as it is in heaven.

Give us this day our daily bread.

And forgive us our trespasses,

as we forgive those who trespass against us.

And lead us not into temptation,

but deliver us from evil.

For thine is the kingdom, and the power, and the glory,

forever. Amen.

* Note to leaders: Obviously, if you use a different version of the Lord's Prayer regularly in your church, use the one your students would be most familiar with.

5 Know Why You Believe

Summary

Having established a firm foundation of belief in God's love, this lesson will explore God's expectations for what we are to do with that love.

Overview

- **Connect** through a choice of activities that will challenge the students to think about how they share what they believe to be true about God.

- **Explore** what Scripture tells us about God's expectations for followers of Christ.

- **Reflect** on barriers that keep us from sharing God's love.

- **Create** a plan for addressing common concerns for nonbelievers.

- **Next,** see where other churches or denominations stand.

Anchor Point

- *Matthew 25:21 — His master replied, "Excellent! You are a good and faithful servant! You've been faithful over a little. I'll put you in charge of much. Come, celebrate with me."*

Supplies

- High-Energy Supplies: index cards with truth and opinion statements written on them

- Low-Energy Supplies: index cards with statement or instructions written on them, or blank

- Chart paper or markerboard with markers

- Student Guides

- Bibles or Bible app

- Pencils/pens

Parent Email

This week your student will be focusing on the importance of sharing their faith with others. For some people, this is not a comfortable scenario; for others, it comes naturally. Natural or not, we are called to share the good news of Jesus Christ with others. Each week we have encouraged you to be part of your student's faith journey. Sharing what you believe about God and why you believe in God is incredibly formational for your student.

Talk with your student:

- Share about a time when you talked with someone about your beliefs in God.

- Share the challenges you have with sharing your beliefs with others.

- Make a commitment to talk about your beliefs with each other to help overcome both of your hesitations.

Leader Notes

Teaching young disciples how to share their beliefs confidently but with emotional intelligence is a daunting and intensive task. As with all the lessons in this study, the foundational pieces of faith-sharing that are covered and reviewed in this lesson will help them in their faith journey.

As always, you should be prepared with examples of times when you were successful in sharing your faith, as well as times when you were less successful.

Theology and Commentary

Parables are an excellent teaching tool that allow the hearer to enter the lesson at his or her own pace. They provide the Holy Spirit opportunity to engage the hearer with conviction, education, support, or encouragement.

While the focus of Matthew 25:14-46 is on the joy and celebration that is found in sharing the love of God with others, this lesson approaches the two parables here through the lenses of accountability and responsibility.

What the expectations are and the consequences of a believer's behavior, however, are open to interpretation. Please note, however, that any interpretation that devalues any human being or condemns others based on human judgment is not a faithful interpretation of God's grace and love that is at the core of our faith and Scripture.

These parables are not directed to the unbelievers, but rather those inside God's household and flock. Therefore, expectation and accountability fell on those who were already part of the community. They are not scare tactics used to subdue unruly children, but boundaries sketched out to define a relationship.

Leader Reflection

Read Matthew 25:1-46.

"Come, celebrate with me" (25:21). This is the joyful invitation we should be offering to others, into the love of our God. All too often, we fall into the trap of equating evangelism with church membership and miss the joy of inviting people into a loving relationship with our friend, Jesus.

We can easily be caught up in the negative consequences of God's accountability and miss the multiple times God invites, praises, and loves. These parables of accountability aren't meant to threaten us into submission. They are supposed to set the boundaries of a relationship with Jesus. Jesus is simply laying out what it looks like to love him.

Holding one another accountable to healthy boundaries is one of the components of a lasting relationship and also one of the hardest aspects of a relationship to manage.

As you are preparing to talk with your students about sharing their faith, start where God starts: a place of invitation, praise, and love.

- What aspects of accountability make you uncomfortable? Why?

- When have you had an experience of being held accountable? What about that experience can you use to help your students?

Be in prayer for your students and your preparation:

- Ask God to forgive the times you have intentionally or unintentionally been stingy sharing love.

- Listen to God's direction for how to balance talking about responsibility, accountability, and love.

- Ask God to fill your students with wisdom and courage to talk with their peers about their faith.

Connect (8 minutes)

High-Energy Option—*Say It with Confidence*

[Before the lesson, count out as many index cards as you have students. On half of the cards, write facts; on the remaining cards, write opinion statements. Examples of facts could include: the sky is blue, and trees make oxygen. Examples of opinion statements could include: summer is the best season, the (insert sports team) are the best, French fries are the best fast food.

Before the students arrive, spread the index cards out, statement up, on a table.]

Say: When I say, "Go," go over to the table and choose an index card. When everyone has a card, each of you will have to read the card aloud to the group. Your job is to convince everyone that you believe what's on that card is true.

Say: If you convince everyone that you believe what you say, you will be able to sit down. If you don't convince everyone you believe what you say, then you'll have to remain standing until everyone has taken a turn. Those left standing will swap cards and get another chance to convince others they believe what they say with a new card.

After everyone is seated, **ask:**

1. What does it feel like for someone to be skeptical of something you believe?

2. What does it feel like to have to say something confidently that you aren't sure you fully believe?

3. What can you do to gain confidence in saying what you believe?

Say something like: Part of believing in Jesus is sharing that belief with others. While we are confident in the truth of the gospel, at times, we are not fully confident in how our truth will be received.

Say: Today we are going to work on sharing our faith with others. This makes some people uncomfortable; for others, it comes naturally. Natural or not, we are called to tell others about God, so we've got to work that out.

Low-Energy Option — *Broken Telephone*

[Before the lesson, write on four index cards the following:

1 — STATEMENT: Jesus is the Savior of the world.

2 — INSTRUCTION: You must share the statement without using any names.

3 — INSTRUCTION: If the person sitting to your right is wearing glasses, you must share the statement without using any words containing the letter "A."

4 — INSTRUCTION: If the person sitting to your right has on shoes with laces, you must share the statement, adding at least one personal pronoun.

Complete the "deck" with as many additional blank index cards as number of students you have in the group.

If you want to play more than once, make more than one statement card. At the end of each round, collect the index cards, removing the old statement card and shuffling in a new statement card, then redistribute the new deck.]

Say: We are going to play a game that I'm almost certain you have all played before. We are going to play Telephone, but it's going to be a little different than what you're expecting. I'm going to hand each of you an index card.

Say: One person will have a statement written on that card. Three other people will have instructions written on their card. The rest of you will have blank cards. If you have the card with the statement, then you will start our game by whispering that statement into the ear of the person to your right.

Say: If you have a blank card, then you will whisper the statement you hear into the ear of the person to your right. If you have a card with instructions on it, you will first listen to the statement whispered into your ear and then, following the instructions on your card, whisper the statement into the ear of the person on your right. Ideally, you would do this without tipping anyone off to the fact you are following the instructions.

Say: The person to the left of the person who started the game will tell the entire group the statement that reaches him/her.

Following the game, **ask:**

1. Who had to follow their instruction card? How did it feel to know you had to intentionally change what someone said to you?

2. How did you feel when someone intentionally changed the statement you told them? How did you know they did it intentionally?

3. Have you ever been in a situation where you had to change how you were going to say something because of the person you were saying it to?

Say something like: For some it comes naturally, and makes others uncomfortable — to believe in Jesus means we are to share that belief with others. Sometimes we must get creative in how we share the truth of the gospel. At times, we must choose our words carefully, so that others can understand what we are trying to say about Jesus.

Explore (13 minutes)

Accountable to Jesus

Say something like: Have you ever known that someone had an expectation of you, but you had no idea what it was? Jesus used parables, often a confusing form of communication, to help his followers understand what was expected of them. There are two parables back-to-back in the Gospel of Matthew that paint a picture of what is expected of Christ's followers.

Say: I'm going to ask you to form two equal groups.

[Give them thirty seconds to form groups, then assign one group Matthew 25:14-30 and the other Matthew 25:31-46. Then, give the following instructions.]

Say: Take five minutes to read the parable silently in your groups. Highlight anything that is confusing or not clear to you. We'll come back to that later.

Say: After everyone has read the passage, as a group take another five minutes to answer the questions that are in the Explore section of your Student Guide. Make sure you write down your answers so that someone from your group can share them with everyone.

Say: As you read your assigned passage, look for three things:

• How were people expected to behave?

• What happens to those who meet the expectations?

• What happens to those who do not meet the expectations?

[After giving ten minutes for the group work, ask each group to share the answers to their questions.]

Say something like: Living up to expectations can be daunting, but most of the time, expectations are for our benefit. God does have expectations for us to love and to share the gospel with others.

[This would be a good place to tell the students what you feel evangelism means in your community and context.]

Say: Telling others about Jesus is what we're called to do. We are called to talk with others about Jesus and provide accountability, encouragement, and support for one another as we learn how.

Say: Accountability isn't about making sure you're following all of the rules and doing things perfectly. Remember from last week, that's not what loving God is about. Holding one another accountable is part of having a healthy relationship. Let's watch a short video about accountability and our faith.

[Play Video 5.]

After the video, **ask:**

• What is the point of accountability?

• How could healthy accountability be turned into unhealthy judgment?

• Why do we feel uncomfortable with accountability?

Reflect (5 minutes)

Say something like: Because sharing our faith is challenging, it is important for us to take time to reflect on our experience doing it so far. Turn to the Reflect section of your Student Guide and follow the prompts listed.

Say: Think about a chance you had to tell someone about your faith. Why didn't you do it?

Ask: What prevented you from talking about God's love?

Say: Write how you wish the conversation had gone instead.

Create (18 minutes)

Say something like: One reason it may be hard to talk about God's love is because we haven't thought through why it is we believe in it. A firm understanding of your "why" is what moves you from passive faith to passionate belief.

Say: To start that process, let's take a minute and list on the board/paper reasons you have heard for why people don't believe in God, and/or why God is not real, and/or why they don't need God in their life.

[Something like these reasons will probably arise.]

- I can be a good person on my own. I can help others without some god telling me to do it.

- I can't believe in a god who would let terrible things happen and lots of people get hurt.

- Science proves that gods don't exist.

After discussion, **say:** Another reason it's hard to talk about God's love is because sometimes we feel defensive when others ridicule or are hostile toward us. So, knowing that these are some of the negative reactions we are going to encounter, let's take some time to prepare ourselves.

Say: Form teams for each reason—you get to select which team you want to be on. In your Student Guide, you will find instructions and a place to record the answers to this next exercise.

Say: Take ten minutes in your teams to think through how you would respond to your issue, using the prompts written for you.

[After ten minutes, ask each group to share their work.]

After all groups have shared, **ask:** How can you use someone's doubt or disbelief to begin a conversation about where God is working in their life?

Ask: Why is it easier to talk about your faith with someone you know is a Christian?

Ask: How do you think a nonbeliever would respond if you started a conversation like this: "I don't know exactly the best way to talk about my faith with you, but I was wondering . . . "

Ask: What is *your* goal for sharing your beliefs with others? What do you think God's goal is for you sharing your beliefs with others?

Next (2 minutes)

Say: Write down one of the problems from the board in your Student Guide. Take fifteen minutes this week and look at a few different denominational websites to see if there is any indication of how the different traditions address the issue. Most of these denominational websites have a "What We Believe" tab or section that will help direct you to some answers.

- What issues do you want to look further into?

- Note a few different ways denominations handle this issue.

- Which way of handling it makes the most sense to you?

Suggested denominational websites:

www.umc.org (The United Methodist Church)

www.ame-church.com (African Methodist Episcopal Church)

www.elca.org (Evangelical Lutheran Church in America)

www.sbc.net (Southern Baptist Convention)

www.abc-usa.org (American Baptist Churches USA)

www.nationalbaptist.com (National Baptist Convention, USA, Inc.)

www.church-of-christ.org/who (Churches of Christ)

www.pcusa.org (Presbyterian Church [USA])

www.episcopalchurch.org (The Episcopal Church)

www.cogic.org (The Church of God in Christ, Inc.)

Say something like: As we end our time together, we are going to pray a dangerous prayer. We are called to offer prayers like this, but we often don't because it may mean God will answer them and we'll have to do something. So, if you have the courage to pray this with me, then I invite you to turn to the Next section in your Student Guide and pray aloud with me. If you're not there yet, that's just fine. Spend this time praying for those who are taking this next faith step. Let's pray.

Prayer

God, send people into our lives who need to know your love. Help us to come together as your followers to exemplify Christ and bring others to want to know Christ for themselves.

God, help me build a caring relationship with someone who needs your love. Help me become the kind of Christlike servant who will open the doors to a life with you.

God, bring me opportunities to talk about my relationship with you. Give me the words to talk about the mysteries of Christ, even if I don't fully understand them.

God, fill us with your Holy Spirit to be the light that leads others to you.

In Jesus' name, we pray. Amen.

6 Hearing God Speak

Summary

The final leg of this journey is understanding that this is not the end of the road, but more lies ahead in our walk with God. This final lesson will help remind students that hearing God often means listening to the words of others, sometimes even strangers.

Overview

- **Connect** through thinking about questions or an affirmation activity.

- **Explore** the call of Rebekah to serve God.

- **Reflect** on how you would react in Rebekah's situation.

- **Create** a story portraying different ways to respond to God's call to serve.

- **Next,** think about the different ways God is calling you to serve now and in the future.

Anchor Point

Genesis 24:57-58 — They said, "Summon the young woman, and let's ask her opinion." They called Rebekah and said to her, "Will you go with this man?"

She said, "I will go."

Supplies

- High-Energy Supplies: chairs, one blindfold

- Low-Energy Supplies: present-day picture of each student from Lesson 1 pasted on its own posterboard, markers

- Student Guides

- Markers or highlighters

- Bibles or Bible app

- Pens/pencils

Parent Email

This is the final week of your student's AFFIRM study. Hopefully, as you have walked with your student through these last weeks, your faith has been strengthened as well as theirs. The life of a disciple calls for constant learning and growth in sharing Christ's love. We hope this study has helped give your student the tools to grow as a disciple of Christ, sharing her or his faith. Though your student is concluding this study, we encourage you to have ongoing conversations about faith, living for Christ, and loving like God. Your influence on your son's or daughter's faith is significant.

Talk with your student . . .

- about what she or he will continue to do to grow his or her faith after the study ends

- about a faith practice he or she liked and one they didn't, and why

- about how you can help your student continue to grow his or her faith and share God's love

Leader Notes

Most of the "conclusive" work of the study should be accomplished by the students during their devotional time. One of the activities in the devotion will be to write personal affirmations of faith. Sharing these as a culmination of the study, either within the group or in the wider congregation, could be definitive for some students. Possible ways to share those affirmations in the group or life of the congregation:

- Ask for students to volunteer to share them during worship

- Ask for permission to print some of the affirmations in the worship bulletin/folder, church newsletter, or on church social media sites.

- Replace the Connect activity with students sharing affirmations with one another.

- Ask students to share their affirmations as the closing prayer time. (Note, this may extend the session significantly.)

Theology and Commentary

Teaching the Bible can be complicated because some of the stories we lift as sacred contain practices we presently find repugnant. The call story of Rebekah is one of those cases in which the cultural practices of the time of the story are incompatible with our present understanding of the gospel. While the custom of purchasing a wife is not a practice common in Western cultures, we are unfortunately familiar with human trafficking, where women are bought and sold.

There are two ways to address the dilemma of celebrating the story of God's people while being faced with practices that are not acceptable in our culture. The first is to ignore the conflict and engage the story for only what we want out of it. This leads to a shallow engagement with God's Word. The second is to acknowledge the injustice in the story, and in current cultures, and explore how God works through an unjust practice to redeem God's people. This second option acknowledges the value and suffering of those who are victims of injustice, without nullifying the impact of our ancestors on our faith.

Genesis 24 has much to teach believers beyond how to interact with complicated cultural norms. This chapter is the longest in Genesis[3], and arguably the most detailed call account in the whole of Scripture. The number of people who are part of Rebekah's call is also significant. From Abraham to his servant to Rebekah to family members and finally back to Rebekah, the contribution of the community in confirming Rebekah's call is not to be overlooked. Also worth noting are instances in which Rebekah had opportunities to turn from God's call. In each of these instances, she chose to say, "I will go."

---

3 Carol Meyers, *Women in Scripture* (Houghton Mifflin Company: 2000), 143

Leader Reflection

Read Genesis 24:1-67 and Joshua 1:1-8.

Hearing God calling you into service can trigger a variety of emotions, from excited anticipation to bone-numbing fear. We can't say with certainty what Rebekah and Joshua felt when God called them to serve, but we can suppose it was somewhere on that spectrum. Where were you on that spectrum when you accepted the call to teach this study? How has this experience impacted how you feel about serving God? What has this experience taught you about listening for God's calling?

God's call to service can lead to a variety of destinations, most of which will not be your final stop. You were called by God to lead these students through this study. This study is coming to a close, but your service to God is not at an end. As you are preparing this final lesson, it is important for you to pause and listen for where God is calling you to serve next.

Be in prayer for your students and your preparation:

- Thank God for the blessings you have received through accepting your call to service.

- Ask God to reveal to you where you are needed to serve next.

- Ask God to reveal to you where God plans for the students in your study to be in service.

Connect (8 minutes)

High-Energy Option — *Twenty-Questions Tag*

[Before the students arrive, arrange chairs in a circle with the seats facing the center of the circle. Use one less chair than the number of students present. Once everyone has arrived, give the following instructions.]

Say: I need a volunteer to start our game in the middle of the circle, with a blindfold on. Everyone else, please find a seat in one of the chairs in the circle.

Say: The person in the middle of the circle is going to pick an object in this room, and those of you in the circle are going to try to guess what object he or she is thinking of. One at a time, you will ask the person in the middle up to twenty yes-or-no questions. If the person says yes, then everyone must get up and find a new seat while the person in the middle tries to tag as many people as possible. The goal of the people sitting in the circle is to guess the object before you get to twenty questions or until all the players are tagged by the person in the middle.

Say: You may not sit in the seat immediately to your right or left. If you are tagged, you remove a chair from the circle and sit on the outside of the game. Those on the outside of the game can give players still in the game questions to ask, but they cannot help players guess the object.

Following the game, **ask:**

- What was the last question you asked, hoping that the answer would be no?

- When was the last time you freaked out when someone answered your questions with a yes?

- Have you ever said yes to something, knowing it would result in chaos? What made you say yes?

Say something like: Today is our last session, and we are going to spend some time exploring what it means to listen for God, and what it means to say yes when God calls us to serve. There are times when we know what God is wanting us to do, so we phrase our questions to God in a way that guarantees a no, such as: "Well, God, you don't want me to fail this test because I went to church, do you?" Other times, we are terrified by what we are saying yes to. For example, "Yes, I will say the blessing at the fundraiser meal for the entire congregation after church." In both scenarios, God continues to be with us until we accept whatever God is asking us to do.

Low-Energy Option—*Affirming Each Other*

[Before the lesson, using the present-day pictures of the students from Lesson 1, paste the picture of each student in the middle of its own piece of posterboard or card stock. Place the posters and markers on tables around the room. As students arrive, give them the following instructions.]

Say: As you walk around the room, you will see the pictures of our class members. I would like each of you to visit each person's picture, and on the space around the picture, write words of support or thanks or praise about that person. Please try to go a little deeper than, "Thanks for the donut." Instead, try saying, "It made me feel special when you gave me the last donut."

[After everyone has written on the posters, give them to their owners and allow time for them to read over the affirmations.]

Following the activity, **ask:**

- Were there any comments on your poster that surprised you? What were they? Why was it surprising?

- Which was more comfortable for you, writing affirmations or reading your affirmations? Why?

- What do you hear God saying to you through the comments on your poster?

Say something like: Today is our last session, and we are going to spend some time exploring what it means to listen for God, and what it means to say yes when God calls us to serve. Oftentimes, we don't hear God because we are waiting for God to speak directly to us. But sometimes, God chooses to guide us through the words and prayers of others.

Explore (12 minutes)

Answer to a Prayer

Say something like: Let's watch a video that tells us a story about a young woman who said yes to God, based on the word of a complete stranger.

[Play Video 6.]

[After playing the video . . .]

Say something like: The custom of taking possession of women and claiming them for marriage, like a piece of property, is not an acceptable way to treat human beings. We need to recognize this unjust treatment both in the present and in the past, but also consider how in the midst of injustice, God calls people to service.

Say: As we explore the story of Rebekah's call to serve God, we realize Rebekah never heard God's voice calling her directly, as Moses and Samuel did. Rebekah only knows God is calling her because another person told her she was an answer to his prayers. There may be times when some of us will hear God speak clearly about what we are supposed to do for God. Others will have to depend on God to speak to and through other people to know what God is asking you to do.

Say: Following God based on the word of someone else is risky. That kind of step requires faith in God and trust in your fellow believer. Rebekah is a shining example of stepping out in faith to follow God's call.

Say: Fear is one of the biggest emotions that prevents us from following God's call. However, having a partner with us helps make following God less scary. We are going to partner together to think through some of the scary parts of Rebekah's calling.

Say: In your Student Guide, you will find a portion of Rebekah's story. I'm going to ask you to take three minutes to read the verses and underline anything said or done that might have made Rebekah scared, nervous, or unsure. I would like you to circle anything said or done that might have given Rebekah strength and courage. When you're done reading, we will all first share the thing said or done that might cause fears, and then share the things said and done that build courage.

[After three minutes to read and respond . . .]

Say something like: What did you notice that might have made Rebekah scared, nervous, or unsure?

[Allow the students time to share their responses. If there is a long silence, you might suggest she didn't know the servant coming to take her away was a stranger.]

Ask:

- Of all the scary situations we named, which one do you think would have required the most trust from Rebekah? Why?

- How do you think people learn to trust God?

Ask: What did you notice that might have given Rebekah strength and courage?

[Allow the students a time to share their responses. You might suggest the gifts given to her family by the servant showed her family was valued just as she was.]

- Are there any of these instances that provided strength or courage for any of the specific fears named earlier?

- How can we recognize God calming our fears?

Reflect (4 minutes)

Say something like: Because each person's journey with
God and call is unique, it is important for you to take time to
consider how you are being called by God on your journey.
Please turn to the Reflect section of your Student Guide and
follow the prompts listed.

Say: Imagine what it would have been like to be Rebekah.

Ask: What kinds of things do you think you would be feeling?

Ask: What questions would you want to ask?

Ask: If someone were to tell you that as an answer to a prayer,
God was calling you to leave your family, who would you want
to talk to before you decided to accept the call? What would
you want to say to them?

Create (16 minutes)

Say something like: I would like us to move now into three groups. In your Student Guides, under the Create section, you will find three numbered prompts of the different ways God calls us and God's goal for the call.

Say: I will give each group a number, and then I would like each group to create a skit demonstrating how they think God would go about accomplishing God's goal.

Say: Think of how the situation might cause fear or uncertainty, and how God would provide courage and strength.

[After ten minutes working together, each group will share their skit or tell their story with everyone.]

Group 1—*Prompt:* A Christian adult advisor is praying a certain student will join a school club to provide a positive Christian example for others in the club.

God's Goal: Students sharing their faith.

Group 2—*Prompt:* A student in a youth group prays that a certain adult will begin to help lead youth group.

God's Goal: For the student and the adult to use their gifts to grow God's kingdom.

Group 3—*Prompt:* A refugee student prays for God to provide her family a church to make them feel more welcome in their new community.

God's Goal: For God's children to share love with the hurt and lonely.

[Allow ten minutes for the groups to form and work on their prompt. Then ask each group to share their skit or story. Following all of the groups sharing . . .]

Ask:

1. In our scenarios, God used the prayers of others to call people to share their faith, use their gifts, and love the hurt and lonely. Why else would God call people into service? *(to right injustice, build a new church, teach the Bible, and so forth)*

- What other scenarios can you think of that God may use someone else to ask *you* to do something?

- Why do you think God sometimes uses other people to show us what God needs done?

- How do you think you tell the difference between God asking YOU to follow a call and God asking you to ask SOMEONE ELSE to follow a call?

Following discussion, **say something like:** God calls each and every one of us to do something for God's kingdom. Some of you will be called to be ministers in God's church. Those called to be pastors have very specific gifts and passions that God has given them to lead the community of faith. Those not called to be pastors still will be called to share the gospel, but just in different ways. Pastors and church teachers are not the only people responsible for sharing God's Word and love; each believer of God has that responsibility.

Next (4 minutes)

Joshua 1:5-6: I will be with you in the same way I was with Moses. I won't desert you or leave you. Be brave and strong, because you are the one who will help this people take possession of the land, which I pledged to give to their ancestors.

Say: Write down three ways God is calling you to be in service.

1 — In the next month

2 — After you graduate high school

3 — When you get a job

Prayer

Blessing Each Other

Say something like: For our closing prayer, each of you will read a passage you select in your Student Guide as a prayer over each person in our group.

Romans 15:5-6 — May the God of endurance and encouragement give you the same attitude toward each other, similar to Christ Jesus' attitude. That way you can glorify the God and Father of our Lord Jesus Christ together with one voice.

Romans 15:13 — May the God of hope fill you with all joy and peace in faith so that you overflow with hope by the power of the Holy Spirit.

2 Corinthians 13:13 — The grace of the Lord Jesus Christ, the love of God, and the fellowship of the Holy Spirit be with you all.

Ephesians 6:23-24 — May there be peace with the brothers and sisters as well as love with the faith that comes from God the Father and the Lord Jesus Christ. May grace be with all those who love our Lord Jesus Christ forever.

1 Thessalonians 3:12-13 — May the Lord cause you to increase and enrich your love for each other and for everyone in the same way as we also love you. May the love cause your hearts to be strengthened, to be blameless in holiness before our God and Father when our Lord Jesus comes with all his people.

2 Peter 3:18 — Grow in the grace and knowledge of our Lord and savior Jesus Christ. To him belongs glory now and forever.

CPSIA information can be obtained
at www.ICGtesting.com
Printed in the USA
LVHW02s0614060718
582846LV00001B/1/P